Reset

ADVENT DEVOTIONS
FOR THE WHOLE FAMILY

The
Seedbed
Daily Text

Reset

ADVENT DEVOTIONS
FOR THE WHOLE FAMILY

Advent

D. WALT

Scripture quotations marked NIV are taken from the Holy Bible, New International Version®, NIV® Copyright © 1973, 1978, 1984, 2011 by Biblica, Inc.™ Used by permission of Zondervan. All rights reserved worldwide. www.zondervan.com The "NIV" and "New International Version" are trademarks registered in the United States Patent and Trademark Office by Biblica, Inc.™ All rights reserved worldwide.

Printed in the United States of America

Cover and page design by Strange Last Name
Page layout by PerfecType

Walt, John David.
 Reset : Advent devotions for the whole family / J.D. Walt. – Frankin, Tennessee : Seedbed Publishing, ©2018.

    pages ; cm. -- (The Seedbed daily text)

    ISBN 9781628244540 (paperback : alk. paper)
    ISBN 9781628244557 (Mobi)
    ISBN 9781628244564 (ePub)
    ISBN 9781628244571 (uPDF)

    1. Advent--Prayers and devotions. 2. Families--Prayers and devotions.
    3. Devotional calendars. I. Title.

BV40.W34 2017   242/.332   2017957113

 Seedbed

SEEDBED PUBLISHING
Franklin, Tennessee
seedbed.com

Contents

Introduction:
Who Is Ready for a Reset?
Welcome to Advent!

What is the most important document in your life?

The Bible. Good answer! But, not exactly. Is it your budget, your bank statement, or, heaven forbid, your e-mail inbox? I say the most important document in life is our calendar. We look at it multiple times a day, every day. The truth of the matter? If I have something I'm supposed to do and it's not on my calendar, it doesn't happen.

We think of calendars as primarily being about our future and what's coming next, but here's the surprising thing: calendars are really all about the past. If you gave me your calendar from last year I could tell you last year's story—where you spent your time, your money, your friends, what you valued. In short, our calendars answer all the big questions: who, what, when, where, and how long? The most defining dates on our calendars are reminders about something that happened somewhere in our past (i.e., birthdays, anniversaries, holidays, etc.). Calendars remind us of our stories by annual reenactments. The future gets framed by what happened in the past.

Calendars were God's idea. Think about it. We aren't two chapters into the Bible and we already have a calendar set around God's vision for time. God creates in six days and rests on the seventh. It's not coincidental that the first thing God says is holy in all of creation is time itself, which ups the ante on this whole calendar conversation. "Then God blessed the seventh day and made it holy, because on it he rested from all the work of creating he had done" (Gen. 2:3).

We are hardly two books into the Bible and God instructs his people to order their calendar around his incredible intervention known as the Passover and the exodus. As the story of Israel unfolded, other holy days would be added to their calendar, creating practical opportunities for annual, immersive reorientation of everything around God, and his provision for the past and his vision for the future.

Are you tracking? Calendars were originally invented to repeatedly reorient people around the reality of God. Sure, our calendars can be filled with sports seasons and hunting seasons and national holidays and observances and a thousand other things. Here's the big question: Of all the calendars we observe, which calendar governs? How does your calendar unveil the vision, unfurl the plan, and unfold the timeline? How does your calendar continually reorient you around the reality of God and his kingdom?

Does the word "Advent" mean anything to you?

For some it conjures up childhood memories of purple candles, wreaths, and chocolate candy calendars.

For others it feels like a bunch of disjointed religious motions the church keeps repeating year after year.

For still others it is simply the on-ramp to Christmas and all Christmas has come to mean (or not mean) across our cultural landscape.

What if I told you Advent is the first month of the year?

But wait! Isn't January the first month of the year? Yes, January is the first month of the Gregorian Calendar, which was the next iteration of the Julian Calendar (as in Julius Caesar). Did it ever occur to you that our months are pretty much named after Roman gods and emperors (i.e., March from Mars, April from Aphrodite, July from Julias, August from Augustus, etc.)?

Advent is the first month of the biblical calendar. It's like a giant Reset button crying out to give us a fresh start again. All of time is marked around the signal event in the history of the world, the coming of Jesus Christ: BC and AD. Advent is the season of the year and the month on the calendar when we prepare to mark the massive reset from BC to AD. That day, of course, is Christmas. Now, if Christmas is truly going to be more than just all the stuff of Christmas, it will be up to us to make it so. This is the purpose of Advent—to remind us of the greatest reset in the history of resets. The strange word means "coming."

It gets even better. Advent not only prepares us to mark the cataclysmic watershed moment in the history of time: the first coming of Jesus Christ. Advent calls us to prepare for the end of time, which will be marked by the second coming of Jesus Christ. Like no other calendar in the world, the biblical calendar is not an endlessly repeating cycle of winter, summer, spring, and fall. The biblical calendar is an actual timeline, a true story line, a calendar with a beginning and an end. Before time there was eternity. Time began with the creation of the world. Time will end, giving way to unfettered eternity, with the second advent of Jesus, the final reset, and the fullness of the new creation.

It brings us to the gospel. With the coming of Jesus Christ, his life, death, resurrection, and ascension, eternal life has invaded time, defeating sin and death, resetting the stage for life, life, and more life. With the coming of the Holy Spirit at Pentecost (another red-letter day on the biblical calendar), eternal life enters the hearts of all who follow Jesus Christ as Savior and Lord. On the night before his death, Jesus offered up a powerful prayer in which he said these words,

> "Father, the hour has come. Glorify your Son, that the Son may glorify you. For you granted him authority over all people that he might give eternal life to all those you have given him. Now this is eternal life: that they know you, the only true God, and Jesus Christ, whom you have sent." (John 17:1–3)

Advent not only marks the great movement from "Before Christ" to "The Year of Our Lord," it signals the beginning of the end of time itself. We live now in the age of grace, the age of the Holy Spirit, the time between the comings of Jesus. Year after year after year, Advent offers a graced season to take stock of our lives, to reorient our priorities, to repent and realign our story with the story of the gospel of Jesus Christ. In short, Advent offers us a chance to hit the Reset button and begin again afresh.

Our calendars need a reset. Our marriages need a reset. Our parenting needs a reset. Our friendships need a reset. Our bodies and souls need a reset. Our churches need a reset. The whole world needs a reset. The good news is the reset is right before us. Will we push the button and get on with it?

What about January?

Yes! We keep January. It's just when the New Year rolls around that we will already be leading the way behind Jesus. January, February, March, and so on is the world we currently live in, but it's not the kingdom we serve. We will be living into a bigger story and marking time with a better calendar, flowing out of a book that will endure forever. And that brings it full circle. The Bible is the most important document in life, so what could be better than to make it our calendar too! After all . . .

> The grass withers and the flowers fall, but the word of our God endures forever. (Isa. 40:8)

And a Holy Advent to you and yours.

For the Awakening,
J. D. Walt
Advent 2017

Reset

ADVENT DEVOTIONS
FOR THE WHOLE FAMILY

In the Beginning

GENESIS 1:1–3, 6–7, 9, 11, 14–15, 20–21, 24, 26–27, 31 | In the beginning God created the heavens and the earth. Now the earth was formless and empty, darkness was over the surface of the deep, and the Spirit of God was hovering over the waters.

And God said, "Let there be light," and there was light. . . .

And God said, "Let there be a vault between the waters to separate water from water." So God made the vault and separated the water under the vault from the water above it. And it was so. . . .

And God said, "Let the water under the sky be gathered to one place, and let dry ground appear." And it was so. . . .

Then God said, "Let the land produce vegetation: seed-bearing plants and trees on the land that bear fruit with seed in it, according to their various kinds." And it was so. . . .

And God said, "Let there be lights in the vault of the sky to separate the day from the night, and let them serve as signs to mark sacred times, and days and years, and let them be lights in the vault of the sky to give light on the earth." And it was so. . . .

And God said, "Let the water teem with living creatures, and let birds fly above the earth across the vault of the sky." So God created the great creatures of the sea and every living thing with which the water teems and that moves about in it, according to their kinds, and every winged bird according to its kind. . . .

And God said, "Let the land produce living creatures according to their kinds: the livestock, the creatures that move along the ground, and the wild animals, each according to its kind." And it was so. . . .

Then God said, "Let us make mankind in our image, in our likeness, so that they may rule over the fish in the sea and the birds in the sky, over the livestock and all the wild animals, and over all the creatures that move along the ground."

So God created mankind in his own image,

in the image of God he created them;

male and female he created them. . . .

God saw all that he had made, and it was very good.

Consider This

So there they were, a teenaged girl named Mary, a virgin, who had a baby in her tummy put there by God, and a young man named Joseph who was to be her husband. Their bags were packed and the donkey loaded and ready. They were leaving Nazareth on the way to Bethlehem. A long trip lay before them.

So what did people do before iPads and Candy Crush to pass the time on long trips? They talked to each other. They told stories. They reminded each other of the history that held them together. One of the ways friends and families and communities grow stronger is to work at staying together in the same story line. I'm imagining that happening between Mary and Joseph on the road to Bethlehem. Now the Bible doesn't tell us any details, but here's how I imagine their conversation going:

MARY: We've got a long trip ahead of us, Joe. What do you think we should talk about?

JOSEPH: I know, Mary. How did we get here anyway?

MARY: Well, Joseph, we have to go all the way back to the beginning. Do you remember how the Torah begins?

JOSEPH: Hang on. I memorized this as a kid. "In the beginning God created the heavens and the earth. Now the earth was formless and empty, darkness was over the surface of the deep, and the Spirit of God was hovering over the waters."

MARY: Yes, and do you remember how God created everything?

JOSEPH: Yes, I think so. He created the whole world by speaking words. I remember hearing the Torah read as a child. It kept saying, "And God said . . ." and after everything he said, the Scriptures said, "And it was so. And God said . . . and it was so. And God said . . . and it was so."

MARY: I get it. I get it, Joe! Everything we see came to be because of God's word.

JOSEPH: Yes, and still—God's word is so much bigger and more powerful than the world. Remember how the great prophet Isaiah wrote, "The grass withers and the flowers fall, but the word of our God endures forever" (40:8)?

MARY: God's word creates light and creates life and creates love and it never fails.

JOSEPH: Yes, Mary, maybe that's what Isaiah meant when he compared the word of God to rain and snow falling from heaven to the earth and bringing life. He said that God's word accomplishes everything he sends it to do (Isaiah 55:10–11).

MARY: That's what's so astonishing about the way God spoke his word to me through that angel, and look at me now. I'm going to have a baby!

JOSEPH: Yep. You can say that again. Pretty astonishing.

MARY: Oh my goodness! It just hit me. The angel's exact words to me were, "The Holy Spirit will come on you, and the power of the Most High will overshadow you" (Luke 1:35). It's just like what happened when he created the world. The Spirit of God overshadowed the formless deep! Do you get it, Joe?

JOSEPH: The Spirit of God spoke the word of God into your very body. It's like creation is happening all over again. It's like a new "In the beginning"! Mary, this is huge! Oops! Not you, Mary—but the word of God.

MARY: Joe, speaking of huge, I think this donkey is getting pretty tired. He needs to be overshadowed by a few trees. We'd better give him a break.

JOSEPH: Okay, Mary, I think I see a rest stop just over the hill.

"The grass withers and the flowers fall, but the word of our God endures forever" (Isa. 40:8). In our family, we practice the Word of God through short litanies. For instance, I will say, "The grass withers and the flowers fall," and my children will respond, "but the word of our God endures forever." It makes for a great way to gather for a meal or to say as I take them to school or before they go to bed at night. We work to find everyday, ordinary ways to lace our days and lives together with God's Word.

PEOPLE, GET READY. JESUS IS COMING!

When Trust Fails, Everything Falls

GENESIS 3:1–8 | Now the serpent was more crafty than any of the wild animals the Lord God had made. He said to the woman, "Did God really say, 'You must not eat from any tree in the garden'?"

The woman said to the serpent, "We may eat fruit from the trees in the garden, but God did say, 'You must not eat fruit from the tree that is in the middle of the garden, and you must not touch it, or you will die.'"

"You will not certainly die," the serpent said to the woman. "For God knows that when you eat from it your eyes will be opened, and you will be like God, knowing good and evil."

When the woman saw that the fruit of the tree was good for food and pleasing to the eye, and also desirable for gaining wisdom, she took some and ate it. She also gave some to her husband, who was with her, and he ate it. Then the eyes of both of them were opened, and they realized they were naked;

so they sewed fig leaves together and made coverings for themselves.

Then the man and his wife heard the sound of the Lord God as he was walking in the garden in the cool of the day, and they hid from the Lord God among the trees of the garden.

Consider This

JOSEPH: Mary, we've got to get back on the road.

MARY: I know. Don't forget to bring those donkey treats.

JOSEPH: You know, Mary, I think a lot about what it would have been like to live in the garden of Eden.

MARY: I know, Joe. Everything was so perfect, wasn't it? God meeting with them in the cool of the evening, taking walks, getting to name every animal under the sun, no cancer or death or even sin in those days.

JOSEPH: I think the three worst words in the entire Bible are, "Now the serpent . . ."

MARY: He will trick you every time if you're not careful. Remember what the serpent said to Eve? "Did God really say you must not eat from any tree in the garden?" It's like I want to yell at her, "Eve! No! God didn't say that."

JOSEPH: Yes, it really threw her off, didn't it? She also seems to have forgotten what God said, though. Remember her reply? "We may eat fruit from the trees in the garden, but God did say, 'You must not eat fruit from the tree that is in the middle of the garden, and you must not touch it, or you will die.'" It's like I want to yell at her too, "Eve! No! God didn't say anything about not touching the tree."

MARY: You know, Joe, God didn't actually say anything to Eve about that tree. God gave that command to Adam before Eve came into the picture. Maybe Adam told her wrong.

JOSEPH: Mary, don't go there.

MARY: The serpent started by trying to confuse Eve about God's word. Then he deceived her with a lie about God's word. Remember that one? "You will not certainly die. For God knows that when you eat from it your eyes will be opened, and you will be like God, knowing good and evil." The serpent got Eve to disobey God by telling her that God's word was not true and could not be trusted.

JOSEPH: You know, Mary, that's one of the things I so admire about you. When God's word came to you from the angel, do you remember what you told him?

MARY: I think I do. It was something like, "Here am I the servant of the Lord. Let it be with me according to your Word."

JOSEPH: When you think about it, you are kind of like a new Eve, Mary. Only you are trusting the truth of God's word and obeying it.

MARY: Oh, Joseph. You would do the same thing. Hang on. You are doing the same thing too, aren't you? Remember that dream you had where God told you not to leave me but to trust him that it would all work out?

JOSEPH: I get it. In ways, we are just like Adam and Eve and God knows we have repeated their mistakes. Let's hope this time we are listening carefully and hearing him rightly.

MARY: Yes, God, please give us ears to hear and a heart to trust you completely.

JOSEPH: That's it, Mary! People don't obey who they can't trust. They might be forced to comply, but obedience actually comes from knowing you can trust because you know you are loved.

MARY: Let's remember that as we are raising this child. Seems like so many parents get that wrong these days, thinking obedience comes from powering down, when it actually comes from being there to catch us when we fall.

JOSEPH: Bingo! That's who our God is; the one who catches us when we fall. The whole world could have ended when Adam and Eve disobeyed God, but God had mercy. Things were never the same after that, but God caught them. They paid a big price for their sin, but God had mercy.

MARY: That's what concerns me about this child. Remember, the angel said we would name him Jesus because he would save his people from their sin. I don't like the sound of that too much. But we trust God, right? I'm just looking forward to the day when that serpent gets the boot!

JOSEPH: Amen. You might give the donkey one of those treats now. We've got to stop soon for the night.

PEOPLE, GET READY. JESUS IS COMING!

3 On the Road Again

GENESIS 12:1–7 | The Lord had said to Abram, "Go from your country, your people and your father's household to the land I will show you.

"I will make you into a great nation,
  and I will bless you;
I will make your name great,
  and you will be a blessing.
I will bless those who bless you,
  and whoever curses you I will curse;
and all peoples on earth
  will be blessed through you."

So Abram went, as the Lord had told him; and Lot went with him. Abram was seventy-five years old when he set out from Harran. He took his wife Sarai, his nephew Lot, all the possessions they had accumulated and the people they had acquired in Harran, and they set out for the land of Canaan, and they arrived there.

Abram traveled through the land as far as the site of the great tree of Moreh at Shechem. At that time the Canaanites were in the land. The Lord appeared to Abram and said, "To your offspring I will give this land." So he built an altar there to the Lord, who had appeared to him.

Consider This

JOSEPH: On the road again. I just can't wait to get on the road again.

MARY: Joe, I think you've got the makings of a song there. I can't say that I agree, though.

JOSEPH: You know, Mary, when you think about it, that's really the song of our people—always on the road again it seems.

MARY: God gave them a great garden with all they needed, yet it didn't seem to be enough for them. If only they had trusted and obeyed God, we wouldn't be making this hard trip to Bethlehem right now, would we?

JOSEPH: You are right, Mary. The human race has sadly become very good at turning God's creation into gory chaos. Can you believe there was a murder in the original family; Cain murdering Abel? Still God held out hope for his people.

MARY: It got so dark, it's like the whole world forgot that God said, "Let there be light." And then that horrible flood.

JOSEPH: But remember Noah and his wife and family and the ark and all those animal families. God saved them.

MARY: Yes, it's like God reset the whole creation again, starting over with a new family.

JOSEPH: It does seem like God likes to start with families, doesn't it?

MARY: But, Joe, that didn't work out too well either. Remember them building that awful tower trying to reach to heaven; trying to be like gods again?

JOSEPH: Yep. God hit the Reset button again, scattering those people all over everywhere and babbling on everywhere they went.

MARY: Joe, I'm starting to see a pattern here. Adam and Eve, Noah and his wife, and remember who came next?

JOSEPH: You are onto something Mary. Of course I remember— Abraham and Sarah. God reset things by beginning with a new family.

MARY: Actually, they weren't that new. They were pretty old, and they didn't have any children either.

JOSEPH: Maybe that was the point. God started again with a man and a woman, without children and too old to have children, and promised to grow a great nation from them; to bless the whole world through them.

MARY: And the first thing he did was to put them on the road again. Soon after that God promised them a new Eden, the Promised Land.

JOSEPH: Years later came the promised child, Isaac. Then came his wife, Rebekah, and their sons, Jacob and Esau, and there's that crazy story about Jacob and Leah and Rachel and their twelve sons becoming the twelve tribes. God picks the unlikeliest families and often the most unlikely people from those families to accomplish the most impossible things.

MARY: Joseph, I think you and I surely fit that "unlikely" part of the pattern.

JOSEPH: And we are definitely in that family line—all the way from Abraham to the tribe of Judah to the house of David, and here we are on our way to Bethlehem, the city of David himself.

MARY: It's so easy to get lost in all the crazy twists and turns of this story of ours and yet it's finding ourselves in this story line over and over again that matters.

JOSEPH: And we haven't even talked about Joseph and Egypt and Pharaoh and Moses. This story of ours gets harder and better all at the same time.

MARY: Uh, Joe, can we save that one for tomorrow? I'm really needing us to pull into that rest stop over there.

PEOPLE, GET READY! JESUS IS COMING!

4 The Beautiful Vision

REVELATION 22:1–5 | Then the angel showed me the river of the water of life, as clear as crystal, flowing from the throne of God and of the Lamb down the middle of the great street of the city. On each side of the river stood the tree of life, bearing twelve crops of fruit, yielding its fruit every month. And the leaves of the tree are for the healing of the nations. No longer will there be any curse. The throne of God and of the Lamb will be in the city, and his servants will serve him. They will see his face, and his name will be on their foreheads. There will be no more night. They will not need the light of a lamp or the light of the sun, for the Lord God will give them light. And they will reign for ever and ever.

Consider This

The world began with the God who gives light. The world will one day begin again with the God who gives light. We must remember the beginning in all its glory. Equally important, we must anticipate the end—which will be the new beginning—in all its glory. People tend to go in one of two directions as relates to the end of the world. They either face enormous apocalyptic anxiety or they tend to ignore it altogether.

There is another alternative; not a third way, but the biblical version, also known as the beatific vision. That's where we are headed this week: a reset of our vision of ultimate reality.

For now, figure out which side of the equation you tend to fall on—anxiety and fear or ignorance and indifference.

To look forward to a new heaven and a new earth is not to wish the present one away. It means, rather, to live in the present with profound hope. True hope means living with neither regrets about the past nor anxieties concerning the future.

PEOPLE, GET READY. JESUS IS COMING!

Being Ready for the End

JOHN 3:16–21 | For God so loved the world that he gave his one and only Son, that whoever believes in him shall not perish but have eternal life. For God did not send his Son into the world to condemn the world, but to save the world through him. Whoever believes in him is not condemned, but whoever does not believe stands condemned already because they have not believed in the name of God's one and only Son. This is the verdict: Light has come into the world, but people loved darkness instead of light because their deeds were evil. Everyone who does evil hates the light, and will not come into the light for fear that their deeds will be exposed. But whoever lives by the truth comes into the light, so that it may be seen plainly that what they have done has been done in the sight of God.

Consider This

Here's a question to get started: What three things do we find in all stories? A beginning, a middle, and an end.

Last week we began with the beginning. We left off right in the middle where we were waiting for Jesus to be born. We will travel all the way to the end. Now the interesting thing about our story is the end is actually a new beginning to the rest of the story, which will never end. The story ends when Jesus comes again, and it begins again with a new heaven and a new earth and it never ends again. This is the final reset.

Knowing how the story will end shows us what we need to do now to be ready. This is where Jesus comes in. Remember the most famous verse in the Bible? John 3:16. Can you say it from memory? "For God so loved the world he gave his one and only Son, that whoever believes in him shall not perish but have eternal life."

This is how God intended it to be from the beginning: eternal life. God never planned for people to die. Remember, Adam and Eve didn't obey God because they didn't trust his word. This was the first sin, and every person who has ever lived since then has been infected by their bad choice. We have all sinned and it means we will all die. It's called the law of sin and death. God never intended this. God is light and life. Sin is darkness and death.

So here's our problem: because of sin we are born into a life that is destined to end in death. Jesus came into the world to do what Adam failed to do: to love God completely, to trust

God fully, and to obey God wholeheartedly. He was like a second Adam. This is how much God loves us. He wants us to trust him completely and obey him wholeheartedly. To do this we must trust and follow Jesus.

God is giving us a second chance to trust him through obeying and following his Son, who has come to save us. This is what it means to be ready when Jesus comes again. More on that to come.

PEOPLE, GET READY. JESUS IS COMING!

Prepared for the Party

MATTHEW 25:1–13 | "At that time the kingdom of heaven will be like ten virgins who took their lamps and went out to meet the bridegroom. Five of them were foolish and five were wise. The foolish ones took their lamps but did not take any oil with them. The wise ones, however, took oil in jars along with their lamps. The bridegroom was a long time in coming, and they all became drowsy and fell asleep.

"At midnight the cry rang out: 'Here's the bridegroom! Come out to meet him!'

"Then all the virgins woke up and trimmed their lamps. The foolish ones said to the wise, 'Give us some of your oil; our lamps are going out.'

"'No,' they replied, 'there may not be enough for both us and you. Instead, go to those who sell oil and buy some for yourselves.'

"But while they were on their way to buy the oil, the bridegroom arrived. The virgins who were ready went in with him to the wedding banquet. And the door was shut.

"Later the others also came. 'Lord, Lord,' they said, 'open the door for us!'

"But he replied, 'Truly I tell you, I don't know you.'

"Therefore keep watch, because you do not know the day or the hour."

Consider This

There are five things we must be clear on as relates to the return of Jesus and the end of the world as we know it.

1. Jesus will return to the earth.
2. It will be a great celebration, akin to a wedding party.
3. No one but God knows when.
4. We do not need to be afraid.
5. We need to be prepared.

PEOPLE, GET READY. JESUS IS COMING!

Becoming a Risk-Taker for Jesus

MATTHEW 25:13–19 | "Therefore keep watch, because you do not know the day or the hour.

"Again, it will be like a man going on a journey, who called his servants and entrusted his wealth to them. To one he gave five bags of gold, to another two bags, and to another one bag, each according to his ability. Then he went on his journey. The man who had received five bags of gold went at once and put his money to work and gained five bags more. So also, the one with two bags of gold gained two more. But the man who had received one bag went off, dug a hole in the ground and hid his master's money.

"After a long time the master of those servants returned and settled accounts with them."

Consider This

Jesus talked a lot about his return and the end of the age. He knew he would be leaving and that it might be a long time before he returned. He used all sorts of ways to describe it. Yesterday he compared the end of the age to the arrival of the bridegroom for a great wedding celebration. The issue was the virgins being prepared by having plenty of oil in their lamps.

Today he says it will be like a man going on a journey who leaves all his wealth with his servants. Note, he didn't give it to them. He entrusted it to them. He retained ownership, but he left them in charge of managing or stewarding it all. He gave each of the servants an amount that he knew they would be capable of managing.

The master's expectation? He intended for his servants to take what he had entrusted to them and turn it into even more. He wanted the servants to take creative risks with the money. A risk means taking the chance of losing everything, but it also means the possibility of a great gain.

Imagine this situation. Jesus says to you, "I'm going to entrust you with one million dollars. This is not your money. It belongs to me, but I want you to take this money and do with it what I would do with it. Really, I want you to take this one million dollars and turn it into ten million blessings or something like that. I'm going to come back. I'm not sure when, but when I do, I want a report on what you were able to do with my money. How did you use my resources to grow my kingdom?"

What would you do with the money?

Here's the lesson: we now live in the midst of this very story. Jesus is the master. We are the servants. Our lives and everything we have has been entrusted to us by Jesus. He will return. We do not know when, but when he does, he will want a report on what we did with all we have been entrusted with to increase his kingdom.

The Preparation for the Return of Jesus Checklist, so far:
• Extra batteries for the flashlight. (check)

- Strategic plan for creatively risking everything for the sake of expanding his kingdom. (in process)

PEOPLE, GET READY. JESUS IS COMING!

The Blessing of Knowing How the Story Ends before It Actually Ends

MATTHEW 25:31–46 | "When the Son of Man comes in his glory, and all the angels with him, he will sit on his glorious throne. All the nations will be gathered before him, and he will separate the people one from another as a shepherd separates the sheep from the goats. He will put the sheep on his right and the goats on his left.

"Then the King will say to those on his right, 'Come, you who are blessed by my Father; take your inheritance, the kingdom prepared for you since the creation of the world. For I was hungry and you gave me something to eat, I was thirsty and you gave me something to drink, I was a stranger and you invited me in, I needed clothes and you clothed me, I was sick and you looked after me, I was in prison and you came to visit me.'

"Then the righteous will answer him, 'Lord, when did we see you hungry and feed you, or thirsty and give you something to drink? When did we see you a stranger and invite you in, or needing clothes and clothe you? When did we see you sick or in prison and go to visit you?'

"The King will reply, 'Truly I tell you, whatever you did for one of the least of these brothers and sisters of mine, you did for me.'

"Then he will say to those on his left, 'Depart from me, you who are cursed, into the eternal fire prepared for the devil and his angels. For I was hungry and you gave me nothing to eat, I was thirsty and you gave me nothing to drink, I was a stranger and you did not invite me in, I needed clothes and you did not clothe me, I was sick and in prison and you did not look after me.'

"They also will answer, 'Lord, when did we see you hungry or thirsty or a stranger or needing clothes or sick or in prison, and did not help you?'

"He will reply, 'Truly I tell you, whatever you did not do for one of the least of these, you did not do for me.'

"Then they will go away to eternal punishment, but the righteous to eternal life."

Consider This

What do sheep and goats have to do with the return of Jesus and the end of time?

Before we go any further, I want to reassure you that when I say things like, "the end of the world," and, "the end of time," I don't mean to scare anyone. The end of time really means the end of time. In other words, we can throw away our watches and clocks because time will be over and we will live in eternity, and eternity never ends. That's what forever means.

As I have noted before, the end of the world means the end of the world as it presently exists in its broken state (i.e., where children have cancer and are sold into slavery and where earthquakes and tsunamis kill thousands of people). When the world as we know it ends, the world as we always hoped it could be begins. This will be the world made right.

This brings me to our text for today and the question about sheep and goats. Part of making the world right means that evil will finally be punished. At the end of time Jesus will return and everyone who ever lived will be raised from the dead. Next will come the judgment. Everyone who is still alive when Jesus comes (along with everyone who was dead) will stand together before the Lord. If you've ever said the Apostles' Creed or the Nicene Creed, this will sound familiar (i.e., "He shall come to judge the quick [living] and the dead.")

Now here's the interesting part. In the end, judgment comes down to one of two decisions. A person either (1) lives forever with God in the new heaven and the new earth or (2) doesn't live forever with God in the new heaven and the new earth. Is a person judged on how much good they have done compared to how much bad they have done? Good question. No. If that were the case, none of us would get to live forever with God in the new heaven and the new earth.

That's where the very good news, also known as the gospel, comes in. Remember? "For God so loved the world that he gave his one and only Son, that whoever believes in him shall not perish but have eternal life" (John 3:16).

Jesus died on the cross and rose from the dead in order to save people from the curse of sin and death. He paid the penalty of sin so that we might have eternal life. The key is that we must put our faith in him. We must believe this good news in our heart of hearts and follow him with our lives.

That's where the sheep and the goats come in. Jesus says the judgment will look something like a shepherd separating sheep from goats. One group will live forever with God in the new heaven and the new earth and one will not. The difference? Do you know what the sign will be of whether a person really trusted in Jesus for their salvation and received his mercy for their sins? The sign will be to see who really showed mercy to other people when they most needed it. Did you feed people when they were hungry? Did you clothe them when they were naked? Did you visit them when they were in prison? Did you care for them when they were sick? Did you welcome in strangers when they had nowhere else to go? Jesus will say, "You thought you were doing it for them, but you were really doing it for me."

People don't live forever with God in the new heaven and the new earth because they showed mercy to people in need. People live forever with God in the new heaven and the new earth because they trusted in Jesus and received his mercy. It just so happens that the people who really received mercy are the same kind of people who show mercy to others. It doesn't come down to what you say but who you have become.

So here's the hard look we need to take at ourselves: Have we placed our faith in Jesus and received his mercy for our failures? Here's how to tell: Are we becoming the kind of people who show mercy and kindness to people who are in need? If we aren't becoming those kind of people, chances are we haven't really trusted in Jesus. In which case, we need to ask ourselves some hard questions.

The good news is that if you are reading this, there is still time. That's what's so amazing about Jesus telling us these things ahead of time. He is giving us a chance to ask ourselves the hard questions now so we can be prepared when the time comes.

PEOPLE, GET READY. JESUS IS COMING!

Never Give Up

LUKE 18:1–8 | Then Jesus told his disciples a parable to show them that they should always pray and not give up. He said: "In a certain town there was a judge who neither feared God nor cared what people thought. And there was a widow in that town who kept coming to him with the plea, 'Grant me justice against my adversary.'

"For some time he refused. But finally he said to himself, 'Even though I don't fear God or care what people think, yet because this widow keeps bothering me, I will see that she gets justice, so that she won't eventually come and attack me!'"

And the Lord said, "Listen to what the unjust judge says. And will not God bring about justice for his chosen ones, who cry out to him day and night? Will he keep putting them off? I tell you, he will see that they get justice, and quickly. However, when the Son of Man comes, will he find faith on the earth?"

Consider This

When the Son of Man comes, will he find faith on earth? Not only is Jesus looking for faith, he's telling us ahead of time what it looks like. In short, faith looks like always praying and never giving up.

This widow went before the judge day after day after day. Her request never changed. It felt like a complete waste of time after a while; like there's no point. Jesus says, just when you are sure it's an impossible situation, stay with it. When it's been two thousand years since he ascended to heaven, be like the widow.

Why? Because while we may be like the widow, Jesus is nothing like the unjust judge. In fact, Jesus is saying he is just the opposite. God is like a loving Father who delights to respond to the cries of his children.

The sign of trust is perseverance, never giving up. Praying always and never giving up. Crying out for justice in this broken world. Pleading for the judge to come and make all things new. That's our calling in the meantime. It's a holy occupation.

PEOPLE, GET READY. JESUS IS COMING!

Let My People Go

EXODUS 1:1–14, 22 | These are the names of the sons of Israel who went to Egypt with Jacob, each with his family: Reuben, Simeon, Levi and Judah; Issachar, Zebulun and Benjamin; Dan and Naphtali; Gad and Asher. The descendants of Jacob numbered seventy in all; Joseph was already in Egypt.

Now Joseph and all his brothers and all that generation died, but the Israelites were exceedingly fruitful; they multiplied greatly, increased in numbers and became so numerous that the land was filled with them.

Then a new king, to whom Joseph meant nothing, came to power in Egypt. "Look," he said to his people, "the Israelites have become far too numerous for us. Come, we must deal shrewdly with them or they will become even more numerous and, if war breaks out, will join our enemies, fight against us and leave the country."

So they put slave masters over them to oppress them with forced labor, and they built Pithom and Rameses as store cities for Pharaoh. But the more they were oppressed, the more they multiplied and spread; so the Egyptians came to dread the Israelites and worked them ruthlessly. They made their lives bitter with harsh labor in brick and mortar and with all kinds of work in the fields; in all their harsh labor the Egyptians worked them ruthlessly. . . .

Then Pharaoh gave this order to all his people: "Every Hebrew boy that is born you must throw into the Nile, but let every girl live."

Consider This

JOSEPH: Mary, we really should be there by now, but all these bathroom stops are making the trip take twice as long.

MARY: Sorry, Joe. I'd say it's your fault, but this isn't exactly your child, is it? So, how much longer did you say till we get there?

JOSEPH: Mary, why don't you be the storyteller today?

MARY: Sure. It was a dark and stormy night . . . only kidding. First, let's remember where we've been so far. We started with God creating the world and everything in it. Then we spoke about Adam and Eve and that crafty serpent and the end of Eden. God reset things again with Abraham and Sarah and he made some pretty astonishing promises to them. From Abraham, we moved to Jacob and then Joseph, and now we have twelve tribes and they all lived in Egypt.

JOSEPH: Egypt started out like a Land of Promise, didn't it?

MARY: Yes, but it later turned into a place of chaos. Those pharaohs crucified our people. Imagine the very people of God reduced to slaves.

JOSEPH: Then Pharaoh made the ultimate move of un-creating. He issued an order to drown all the Israelite baby boys in the Nile River.

MARY: Isn't it amazing, Joseph, how God started to save his people through a tiny baby named Moses? His parents kept him as long as they could hide him, and one day they built a small boat—an ark, if you will—made of reeds and held together by tar. They put him in the little boat and floated it out into the Nile.

JOSEPH: Yes, and isn't it like God to have Pharaoh's daughter rescue this baby and for the future deliverer of Israel to grow up in the palace of the oppressor.

MARY: Joseph, has it occurred to you yet that this baby in my belly, whom we will name Jesus, will be the way God starts to save the world for the last time? He starts with a baby.

JOSEPH: Go on. And can we pick up the pace just a bit?

MARY: With the donkey?

JOSEPH: No, Mary, with the story!

MARY: Okay, the boy grew up. He fled Egypt in fear of his life. Forty years later he's wandering around with a herd of sheep and he came across a mysterious bush. It's on fire, but it was not being burned up. God spoke to him there, calling him to "Set my people free!" Moses went to Pharaoh and nine plagues later they were sacrificing lambs as the main course of the Passover Feast and smearing their blood over their doors. Next thing you know, Moses was leading God's people through the Red Sea on dry ground.

JOSEPH: As a baby he was saved from the Nile and now as a man he was being delivered through the sea. And don't you love it when the creation obeys the Creator like that? Even the wind and the waves obey God.

MARY: So God delivered his people through Moses' faithfulness out of Egypt, the land of slavery, and on to the Promised Land. But there was a small problem.

JOSEPH: I remember. They didn't trust God could keep his promise.

MARY: There it is again. When trust fails, everything falls. God let the hard-hearted generation wander around in that desert for forty years.

JOSEPH: That's another amazing thing about our God, Mary. He will wait out a hard-hearted generation only to turn around and keep the promise to their children.

MARY: That's right. Obedience is inspired by trust, and trust is won by love.

JOSEPH: Time to wrap, Mary.

MARY: Really, Joseph, you want me to just skip Mount Sinai and the Ten Commandments and the golden calf party and the manna from heaven and the water from the rock and the construction of the tabernacle and the ark of the covenant? Okay, have it your way. My mother was right, you never really know a person until you take a road trip with them.

So forty years later, they entered into the Promised Land, a land flowing with milk and honey, and they lived happily ever after. And if you believe that, I've got some oceanfront property in Babylon I'll give you a deal on.

I'll leave it with this for the day—God keeps promises. It's who he is. Let's just keep praying for this baby, Jesus, that he will have the courage of Moses and be mighty to save as God has promised.

PEOPLE, GET READY. JESUS IS COMING!

Encourage One Another with These Words

ACTS 1:7–11 | He said to them: "It is not for you to know the times or dates the Father has set by his own authority. But you will receive power when the Holy Spirit comes on you; and you will be my witnesses in Jerusalem, and in all Judea and Samaria, and to the ends of the earth."

After he said this, he was taken up before their very eyes, and a cloud hid him from their sight.

They were looking intently up into the sky as he was going, when suddenly two men dressed in white stood beside them. "Men of Galilee," they said, "why do you stand here looking into the sky? This same Jesus, who has been taken from you into heaven, will come back in the same way you have seen him go into heaven."

1 THESSALONIANS 4:16–18 | For the Lord himself will come down from heaven, with a loud command, with the voice of the archangel and with the trumpet call of God, and the dead in Christ will rise first. After that, we who are still alive and are left will be caught up together with them in the clouds to meet the Lord in the air. And so we will be with the Lord forever. Therefore encourage one another with these words.

Consider This

When Jesus ascended into heaven, the angels told his followers he would be returning to the earth in the same way they saw him leave. Of course, they all expected that it might happen a week or so later. Years passed and he still hadn't returned. People began to be concerned about their loved ones who had died. What would become of them when Jesus returned? Paul wrote these words to the church at Thessalonica to reassure them everything would be okay. I love how Paul closed by telling them to "encourage one another with these words." How about you? Have you ever encouraged anyone with these words? Has anyone ever encouraged you with these words? I think my answer to both questions would be a no.

Here's the challenge: let's commit to memory the words of 1 Thessalonians 4:16–18 and find ways to encourage one another with them. I am going for it. Will you join me? It's been so long since he came that one can become discouraged about his second coming. I know that has been the case for me at times. Then I remember what the apostle Peter had to say about the waiting:

> But do not forget this one thing, dear friends: With the Lord a day is like a thousand years, and a thousand years are like a day. The Lord is not slow in keeping his promise, as some understand slowness. Instead he is patient with you, not wanting anyone to perish, but everyone to come to repentance. (2 Pet. 3:8–9)

For us it seems like it's been something like two thousand years we've been waiting on his return, but from the Lord's perspective, it's only been a couple of days.

We've got good work to do while we wait; namely, sharing the good news with others now. Our focus has been keeping the vision of the end before us in the now. Being prepared— extra batteries for the flashlights, creative risk-taking with all he has entrusted us with while he is away, always praying, and never, ever, ever giving up.

PEOPLE, GET READY. JESUS IS COMING!

Aligning with the True Story

2 PETER 3:8–14 | But do not forget this one thing, dear friends: With the Lord a day is like a thousand years, and a thousand years are like a day. The Lord is not slow in keeping his promise, as some understand slowness. Instead he is patient with you, not wanting anyone to perish, but everyone to come to repentance.

But the day of the Lord will come like a thief. The heavens will disappear with a roar; the elements will be destroyed by fire, and the earth and everything done in it will be laid bare.

Since everything will be destroyed in this way, what kind of people ought you to be? You ought to live holy and godly lives as you look forward to the day of God and speed its coming. That day will bring about the destruction of the heavens by fire, and the elements will melt in the heat. But in keeping with his promise we are looking forward to a new heaven and a new earth, where righteousness dwells.

So then, dear friends, since you are looking forward to this, make every effort to be found spotless, blameless and at peace with him.

Consider This

As we continue in this time of Advent, let's take stock of where we are. In Week One we reset our story line to coincide with the big story: Creation. Israel. Jesus. Church. New creation.

We have reset our vision of the end of all things broken and the beginning of all things made new, and we explored what it means for us to be prepared and ready.

In summary, we know where we are in the big story. We live in the age of the Holy Spirit, in the era of the church. We live in the time between the first and second coming of Jesus. We understand what it means to be prepared for his return. The big question is: What now?

Our text today picks up where we left off yesterday, asking the critical question: What kind of people ought you be? Answering this question and reordering our lives accordingly is what repentance is all about.

Our big problem? Our lives are aligned with the wrong story: the story of sin and death. Repentance means restoring or re-story-ing our lives according to the story of light and life. Jesus is the light of the world. He is the resurrection and the life. He is the Alpha and the Omega; the Savior and Lord. Repentance is all about following him. He is the way.

PEOPLE, GET READY. JESUS IS COMING!

Priority, Not Priorities

MATTHEW 6:33 | But seek first his kingdom and his righteousness, and all these things will be given to you as well.

Consider This

There are priorities, and then there is priority. The secret to life is knowing the difference. I used to think that life went best when I had my priorities ordered properly. It usually went something like God first, family second, me third. I am learning the secret that life goes best when I have a priority rather than priorities. What do I mean by this?

Today's text, while not a traditional Scripture for Advent, makes it clear.

Seek first the kingdom of God and his righteousness, and all these things will be added to you. Notice what's missing? We have a "first" but no "second." That means we don't have priorities; only a priority. The priority is the kingdom of God and his righteousness. No matter what I'm doing, where I am, or who I'm with, I can seek God's kingdom and his righteousness.

So what does it mean to seek his kingdom and righteousness? This is practically what the New Testament is all about. A good place to start is Matthew 5–7 and Jesus' great kingdom manifesto (a.k.a. the Sermon on the Mount). In short, to seek the kingdom of God is to live our lives as though Jesus were in charge.

So what does this have to do with repentance? Good question. The problem is with the way we define repentance. We want to make it pretty much about turning away from bad behavior. Repentance is bigger than that. The word actually means something like making a 180 degree turn; an about-face.

So what if repentance is actually more about what we turn toward than what we are turning away from?

I think repentance begins not with behavior but with priority. When we focus on behavior we can't help but focus on ourselves. When we focus on priority we are focusing on something beyond ourselves. True repentance begins by resetting our focus on the person of Jesus Christ.

That seems like exactly what we want to be doing in Advent, doesn't it? And when we get our priority right, notice what happens to "all these things."

PEOPLE, GET READY. JESUS IS COMING!

The Lord Lifts Up

PSALM 146:1–10 | Praise the LORD.

Praise the LORD, my soul.

I will praise the LORD all my life; I will sing praise to my God as long as I live. Do not put your trust in princes, in human beings, who cannot save. When their spirit departs, they return to the ground; on that very day their plans come to nothing. Blessed are those whose help is the God of Jacob, whose hope is in the LORD their God.

He is the Maker of heaven and earth, the sea, and everything in them—he remains faithful forever. He upholds the cause of the oppressed and gives food to the hungry. The LORD sets prisoners free, the LORD gives sight to the blind, the LORD lifts up those who are bowed down, the LORD loves the righteous. The LORD watches over the foreigner and sustains the fatherless and the widow, but he frustrates the ways of the wicked.

The LORD reigns forever, your God, O Zion, for all generations.

Praise the LORD.

Consider This

Advent is the perfect time to reset our priorities. If you read yesterday's entry, you learned that we don't need priorities if we have one priority. The one priority for the follower of Jesus is to seek first the kingdom of God and his righteousness.

It's one of the reasons I love Psalm 146. There's a phrase tucked right into the middle of this psalm that has become a favorite antiphonal refrain between one of my closest friends and me. And speaking of antiphonal refrains, they make an excellent way to practice Scripture with other people. We have a few we use around the house frequently as a family. Every morning as I let my children out of the car and send them into their schools I say, "I love you, LORD," and they respond, "my strength" (Ps. 18:1). This summer as we worked with the Beatitudes in the Sermon on the Mount, we would practice them using this "Bible hack" (a better term for antiphonal refrain). I would say, "Blessed are the poor in spirit," and they would say, "for theirs is the kingdom of heaven" (Matt. 5:3). I would say, "Blessed are those who mourn," and they would say, "for they will be comforted" (Matt. 5:4), and on we would go. It's actually a lot of fun and it offers a natural way to "rememberize" Scripture.

Note: *Rememberize* is an ingenious word coined by one of my children who was trying to say "memorize" at the time. To rememberize something is to commit something to memory slowly over the course of time rather than by cramming it all in at once. While memorizing can be effective, it often only sticks around in the short-term memory. Rememberizing has a way of getting the Word deep inside where it finds its way to our memory for the long haul. It's how people with Alzheimer's are still able to sing the old hymns when they can't even remember their name.

It brings me back around to Psalm 146 and the little phrase that led me to the rabbit trail of the practice of rememberizing. The little phrase my friend and I enjoy speaking back and forth to one another is this: one of us will say, "The LORD lifts up," and the other will respond, "those who are bowed down" (v. 8). It's our way of reminding one another of our priority.

Remember, repentance is whatever it takes to get our lives back to the priority of seeking first the kingdom of God and his righteousness. I find this little phrase, "The LORD lifts up those who are bowed down," to be the beginning point of repentance. Repentance is the essential posture of humility and the pathway to true humanity. It's a mark of mature faith.

"The LORD lifts up" . . . your turn.

PEOPLE, GET READY. JESUS IS COMING!

The Mind-Set of Jesus

PHILIPPIANS 2:1–11 | Therefore if you have any encouragement from being united with Christ, if any comfort from his love, if any common sharing in the Spirit, if any tenderness and compassion, then make my joy complete by being like-minded, having the same love, being one in spirit and of one mind. Do nothing out of selfish ambition or vain conceit. Rather, in humility value others above yourselves, not looking to your own interests but each of you to the interests of the others.

In your relationships with one another, have the same mindset as Christ Jesus:

Who, being in very nature God, did not consider equality with God something to be used to his own advantage; rather, he made himself nothing by taking the very nature of a servant, being made in human likeness. And being found in appearance as a man, he humbled himself by becoming obedient to death—even death on a cross!

Therefore God exalted him to the highest place and gave him the name that is above every name, that at the name of Jesus every knee should bow, in heaven and on earth and under the earth, and every tongue acknowledge that Jesus Christ is Lord, to the glory of God the Father.

Consider This

Picking up where we left off yesterday, I say, "The LORD lifts up" and you say, "_____."

Advent is a grace-filled annual opportunity to hit the Reset button on life. It's a great time to reset our story line and our vision on ultimate things, which leads to a reset of our priority. This makes Advent about repentance, which is not commonly associated with chestnuts roasting over an open fire. Repentance means whatever it takes to reset our priority on seeking first the kingdom of God and his righteousness.

Back to our opener: "The LORD lifts up those who are bowed down" (Ps. 146:8). So what does it mean to "bow down"? Thanks for asking. Take a look at today's text. In a word, it looks like humility. The problem with humility is that the minute we think we are being humble, we can be sure we aren't. The only way to be humble is to literally fix our eyes on Jesus and follow him every step of the way. Today's text casts the vision. It is becoming self-forgetful. It is to value others over ourselves, to look to others' interests. It looks like love. Bowing down looks like the mind-set of Jesus Christ.

If ever there were a text made for "rememberizing," it is this one. These words actually made up part of one of the first songs the church ever sang. If only we knew the original tune. I think our lives are meant to be the tune.

Here are some questions for the day: Is my life singing this song? Where did I put others ahead of myself yesterday? Where might I do it today? Remember, you can't be humble by yourself. Humility can only be realized in relationship with others. Humility is not thinking less *of* yourself; it is thinking less *about* yourself. The only way to think less about yourself is to think more about others. The great thing about humility, the practice of bowing down, is that there are endless opportunities to try again.

PEOPLE, GET READY. JESUS IS COMING!

16 Imagine These Possibilities

1 THESSALONIANS 5:23–24 | May God himself, the God of peace, sanctify you through and through. May your whole spirit, soul and body be kept blameless at the coming of our Lord Jesus Christ. The one who calls you is faithful, and he will do it.

Consider This

What happens to a person when their life finally lands on a singular priority? What does it look like when a person ceases to have so many competing and conflicting priorities and life comes down to one thing? It's not that they cease everything else in their lives in order to be more involved in church. No! What happens is that their formerly conflicting and competing priorities all become infused with that singular priority. When this happens, no matter how busy a person may be, no matter how many involvements and commitments and activities they may be engaged in, everything becomes infused with a singular sense of priority and focus. Life becomes aligned and no matter how complex things may look on the outside, on the inside it feels like simplicity.

In fact, the more focused one's priority becomes, the more diverse and interesting their life becomes. Unfortunately, we have lived through a long season of history where the church didn't know how to respond when this kind of priority seized a person's life. The default response of the church to a person whose life had become infused by the Holy Spirit was to steer them toward becoming a member of the clergy. It would be akin to channeling every athlete who shows above-average commitment and skill on the field into coaching. The church needs far fewer coaches and a lot more players.

Staying with the sports metaphor, today's text shows us the possibility of what a real player can look like in this game. It describes what being in the zone is like. It looks like God working in your life at such a deep and profound and yet ordinary level that you become charged with the supernatural substance of the Holy Spirit. In other words, you become holy. Now, the problem with the word "holy" is it has unfortunately become a synonym for "religious." We must bust these myths! Becoming holy actually means leaving religious behind. It means becoming the kind of person whose presence is touched with the presence of God, whose heart beats goodness, whose eyes radiate kindness, whose mind exudes creativity, whose hands create things that will last, whose words are charged with encouragement, whose love becomes brilliant. In short, holiness means a compellingly beautiful life. Imagine the possibilities of this.

Who doesn't want that? This is what being "sanctified" (the biblical word for "made holy") through and through means. It happens to those whose priority is seeking first the kingdom of God and his righteousness. This is where real repentance (realignment) always leads.

"The one who calls you is faithful, and he will do it" (1 Thess. 5:24).

PEOPLE, GET READY. JESUS IS COMING!

17 The Kings and the King

1 KINGS 16:29–31 | In the thirty-eighth year of Asa king of Judah, Ahab son of Omri became king of Israel, and he reigned in Samaria over Israel twenty-two years. Ahab son of Omri did more evil in the eyes of the Lord than any of those before him. He not only considered it trivial to commit the sins of Jeroboam son of Nebat, but he also married Jezebel daughter of Ethbaal king of the Sidonians, and began to serve Baal and worship him.

1 KINGS 18:15–21 | Elijah said, "As the Lord Almighty lives, whom I serve, I will surely present myself to Ahab today."

So Obadiah went to meet Ahab and told him, and Ahab went to meet Elijah. When he saw Elijah, he said to him, "Is that you, you troubler of Israel?"

"I have not made trouble for Israel," Elijah replied. "But you and your father's family have. You have abandoned the Lord's commands and have followed the Baals. Now summon the people from all over Israel to meet me on Mount Carmel. And bring the four hundred and fifty prophets of Baal and the four hundred prophets of Asherah, who eat at Jezebel's table."

So Ahab sent word throughout all Israel and assembled the prophets on Mount Carmel. Elijah went before the people and said, "How long will you waver between two opinions? If the LORD is God, follow him; but if Baal is God, follow him."

But the people said nothing.

Consider This

JOSEPH: Good morning, Mary. I think I'll take over the story-telling today. We've only got a couple of days until we get to Jerusalem, and at the rate we are going it will be Christmas before we're done.

MARY: Christmas? What is that?

JOSEPH: Uh, I'm not sure where that came from.

MARY: So remember where we left off? We went from Moses and the enslavement of Israel in Egypt to the Promised Land flowing with milk and honey. All in all, a forty-year trip.

JOSEPH: Okay, so today let's talk about the kings and prophets of Israel.

MARY: My favorite king and prophet story is the one about King Ahab and Elijah and that wicked witch of the west, Jezebel.

JOSEPH: Let's remember who is who in these stories. In those days, there were priests who spoke to God for the people. There were prophets who spoke to the people for God. Then there were the kings whose job it was to humbly rule the people with the very justice and mercy of God. They were supposed to lead the nation to worship and serve the one and only true God.

MARY: What I remember most is how a king's reign was summed up in the Bible in just a few words.

JOSEPH: Yep. A king either got a thumbs-up or a thumbs-down and it came down to this question: Did they do what was right in the eyes of the Lord or did they do what was evil in the eyes of the Lord?

MARY: Right. Even more specific, it came down to if they worshiped and led the people to worship the true God or Baal or some other false god.

JOSEPH: When kings were doing evil in the eyes of the Lord, God would send a prophet to confront them and call them back to God. Evil kings hated God's prophets.

MARY: But wasn't a prophet God's way of giving the king a second chance?

JOSEPH: You're right, Mary, and sometimes a third and fourth chance.

MARY: So why did all those kings of Israel turn to other gods to care for them?

JOSEPH: Great question. It all comes back to trust. They did not trust the one true God. Remember, when trust fails, everything falls.

MARY: I'm beginning to see a theme.

JOSEPH: Israel had quite a few kings over the years, beginning with Saul, and they mostly did evil in the sight of the Lord. But do you remember God's favorite king?

MARY: Please, Joe. Don't insult me. Everyone knows that was King David. God said of David that he was a man after God's own heart (see Acts 13:22).

JOSEPH: Oh my goodness, Mary! It just hit me. What was it that the angel said to you about David?

MARY: He said, "The Lord God will give him the throne of his father David, and he will reign over Jacob's descendants forever; his kingdom will never end" (Luke 1:32–33). Wow, Joseph! I heard it at the time, but it's hitting me even harder now. This baby will be born a king! And we are headed to the city of David.

JOSEPH: Mary, do you remember when King David brought the ark of the covenant, the dwelling place of God, into the city of Jerusalem? We are on that same road. Mary, do you get what this means?

MARY: It's like we are the ark of the covenant. Joseph, we are *carrying* God! And we are riding on a donkey.

JOSEPH: That's heavy stuff, Mary. We need to pray.

MARY: Agreed. Stop the donkey!

PEOPLE, GET READY. JESUS IS COMING!

Don't Waste Your Life

HEBREWS 12:1–2 | Therefore, since we are surrounded by such a great cloud of witnesses, let us throw off everything that hinders and the sin that so easily entangles. And let us run with perseverance the race marked out for us, fixing our eyes on Jesus, the pioneer and perfecter of faith. For the joy set before him he endured the cross, scorning its shame, and sat down at the right hand of the throne of God.

Consider This

Do you realize Jesus' very first sermon was only three sentences; a mere seventeen words?

"The time has come," he said. "The kingdom of God has come near. Repent and believe the good news!" (Mark 1:15). In that short span, he lifts high the priority through a clarion call to movement: "But seek first his kingdom and his righteousness, and all these things will be given to you as well" (Matt. 6:33).

Today's text echoes, no, it amplifies the priority in the clearest of terms. The many-ness and much-ness of priorities hinder us. We must throw them off. The distraction of sin entangles us. We must throw it off. This is what it means to repent. It's about discarding the good for the sake of the best and ditching the bad for the sake of the glorious.

Repentance, contrary to popular opinion, has absolutely nothing to do with shame-laden, self-absorbed, behavior-management approaches. Repentance is about fixing our gaze on the Beautiful One . . . every single day. And when something gets in the way of that, which it will, it means recovering a clear line of sight and going for the kingdom again. There's absolutely no room for shame and condemnation and all the other garbage that gets passed off as the Christian faith.

While I don't always see eye-to-eye with author and leader John Piper, I do respect him deeply. Something I have heard him say on repeated occasions completely captures the essence of what reset and priority and repentance means. He put it this way, "Don't waste your life!" There are so many good things and bad things to waste a life on. The only way to avoid it is to give ourselves in all things to the One who will give us everything. The Beautiful One—Jesus.

So what does it mean to keep our eyes fixed on him? It's not mustering up some kind of warm fuzzy spiritual feeling of devotion. It doesn't mean becoming a religious zealot. It doesn't mean becoming one of those holier-than-thou people. To keep our eyes fixed on him means becoming his student, a lifelong learner of him. We have an extraordinary record written down in a book of his preexistence, incarnation, birth, life, words, deeds, miracles, signs, betrayal, suffering, passion, death, burial, resurrection, teaching, ascension, and promised return.

To fix our eyes on him means to make him our singular priority by seeking him, studying his every move, hanging on his every word, marveling at his every work, beholding the frailty of his humanity when he is washing feet, bowing at the majesty of his divinity when he is raising the dead, following closer, closer, closer until our eyes develop the capacity to see him in the hungry and the stranger and the prisoner and the homeless . . . and until our lives begin to take on the Holy Spirit–infused skill of imitating him, improvising on his ways, taking on his mind-set, losing ourselves in his mercy, and finding our lives through his faith. He is the pioneer, the perfecter. He will do it.

This is what it looks like to fix our eyes on him. It means to be fixated on the Beautiful One.

PEOPLE, GET READY. JESUS IS COMING!

19 Putting on the Armor of Light

ROMANS 13:11–14 | And do this, understanding the present time: The hour has already come for you to wake up from your slumber, because our salvation is nearer now than when we first believed. The night is nearly over; the day is almost here. So let us put aside the deeds of darkness and put on the armor of light. Let us behave decently, as in the daytime, not in carousing and drunkenness, not in sexual immorality and debauchery, not in dissension and jealousy. Rather, clothe yourselves with the Lord Jesus Christ, and do not think about how to gratify the desires of the flesh.

Consider This

Okay, so I got ahead of myself. There was one more classic Advent repentance text I wanted to share before we get back on the donkey and cruise into Bethlehem for the big day.

I have always loved this text shared above. The imagery of the armor of light captures me. Repentance looks like putting on the armor of light. As John teaches us in his famous sermon:

> Dear friends, I am not writing you a new command but an old one, which you have had since the beginning. This old command is the message you have heard. Yet I am writing you a new command; its truth is seen in him and in you, because the darkness is passing and the true light is already shining. (1 John 2:7–9)

Remember in John's Gospel, after Jesus washed his disciples' feet, he said to them, "A new command I give you: Love one another. As I have loved you, so you must love one another. By this everyone will know that you are my disciples, if you love one another" (John 13:34–35).

As Jesus took off his outer robe and stooped to wash their feet, the Holy Spirit was armoring him in light.

> Anyone who claims to be in the light but hates a brother or sister is still in the darkness. Anyone who loves their brother and sister lives in the light, and there is nothing in them to make them stumble. But anyone who hates a brother or sister is in the darkness and walks around in the darkness. They do not know where they are going, because the darkness has blinded them. (1 John 2:9–11)

Again in the celebrated fifteenth chapter of John's gospel, Jesus brings it all down to one command. He said, "My command is this: Love each other as I have loved you. Greater love has no one than this: to lay down one's life for one's friends" (vv. 12–13). As Jesus was stripped of his robe and nailed to a cross, the Holy Spirit was armoring him in light.

It strikes me as the simple logic of an obvious insight: if there is only one command, there is only one sin. If the one command is to "love each other as I have loved you," the one sin would be the failure to "love each other as I have loved you."

Sin is always personal and always relational. Sin is never private and never individual. Sin always wants to hide alone. Love always wants to make itself known to others. Sin is darkness. Love is light. Sin is death. Love is life. Repentance is the life of love breaking forth in light. It's walking in the light in the armor of light.

Sin can no longer be thought of as a personal moral failure or an individual's bad behavior. It is far worse than this. Sin is the failure of love and it always does violence to someone else. Sin blinds us to others by deceiving us into believing that our sin is about us.

To regain our priority, to seek the kingdom of God and his righteousness, to have the mind of Christ in us, to keep our eyes fixed on Jesus, to put on the armor of light . . . all of this and more comes from the simple, consistent, and continuous act of repentance, which is turning toward love. Let's give John the last word before Bethlehem.

Dear friends, let us love one another, for love comes from God. Everyone who loves has been born of God and knows God. Whoever does not love does not know God, because God is love. This is how God showed his love among us: He sent his one and only Son into the world that we might live through him. This is love: not that we loved God, but that he loved us and sent his Son as an atoning sacrifice for our sins. Dear friends, since God so loved us, we also ought to love one another. No one has ever seen God; but if we love one another, God lives in us and his love is made complete in us. (1 John 4:7–12)

Real repentance always reveals holy love. And it's always as close as the person closest to you right now. Time to armor up.

PEOPLE, GET READY. JESUS IS COMING!

It's What We Do

LUKE 2:1–5 | In those days Caesar Augustus issued a decree that a census should be taken of the entire Roman world. (This was the first census that took place while Quirinius was governor of Syria.) And everyone went to their own town to register.

So Joseph also went up from the town of Nazareth in Galilee to Judea, to Bethlehem the town of David, because he belonged to the house and line of David. He went there to register with Mary, who was pledged to be married to him and was expecting a child.

Consider This

God works out his plans, no matter what.

Something tells me Joseph and Mary had no idea they were going to Bethlehem in order to fulfill biblical prophecy given hundreds of years earlier.

Something tells me they thought they were headed to Bethlehem because Caesar required it.

Something tells me they knew something big was going on with this baby to be born, yet I don't think they had the slightest conception of the magnitude of it all.

They were doing their best to be faithful to God and get along in the world at the same time. Though Mary carried the Lord of heaven and earth in her womb, the lordship of Caesar seemed to carry the day.

Isn't this how life is? We do our best to be faithful to God and get along in the world at the same time? And in the midst of that, God works out his plans. He uses the power of Caesar to fulfill his own prophecy.

Something tells me things were definitely not going according to plan for Mary and Joseph. They had no idea things were working out perfectly, just as God intended. Something tells me it took them years to come to that conclusion themselves.

That's how life is. Things don't seem to go our way, yet God's ways work out. Our lives aren't where we thought they would be by now, yet somehow God has us exactly where he wants us. Because our best laid plans failed, his purposes prevailed. It will take years for us to see it.

Something tells me somewhere along the way Mary and Joseph "rememberized" Proverbs 3:5–6.

We are working on that one at our house. You probably remember it, as it is one of the classics: "Trust in the Lord with all your heart and lean not on your own understanding; in all your ways submit to him, and he will make your paths straight."

We do not understand the ways of God, and so we must not trust our understanding. We trust God with all our hearts. We acknowledge God in all of our ways. That's who we are. That's what we do.

PEOPLE, GET READY. JESUS IS COMING!

Perceiving the Unseen

LUKE 2:8–9 | And there were shepherds living out in the fields nearby, keeping watch over their flocks at night. An angel of the Lord appeared to them, and the glory of the Lord shone around them, and they were terrified.

Consider This

What do you think happened that night on the outskirts of Bethlehem? Did those angels fly in for the occasion? And if so, where did they come from? Heaven? Where is that?

Or did God pull back the veil of the cosmos, giving us a glimpse of what ultimate reality looks like? What if heaven isn't some ethereal, far-off place somewhere "up there"? What if heaven is pressing in on the walls of the universe, hovering all about us?

What if that's what it means when Jesus says the kingdom of heaven is at hand? It's right here, right now, ready to break in.

What if that night, when the Son of God was born in Bethlehem, the Holy Spirit blew a hole in the side of the universe and the kingdom of heaven came flooding in? Wouldn't that explain the phenomenon of the glory of the Lord shining all around them?

What if those angels had been there all along? That's what John seems to have seen in his vision we know as Revelation; a multitude of the heavenly host praising God and singing.

That's what Isaiah said he saw in his celebrated vision. And just like those shepherds, it terrified him.

What if those angels are still here right now hovering just on the other side of the veil?

What if the issue is not their invisibility but our blindness? What if the problem is we don't have eyes to see?

What if we could live out our everyday, ordinary lives with that kind of extraordinary sensitivity; the capacity to sense the unseen?

I think this is one of the more subtle, yet no less spectacular, lessons of that first Christmas; the utterly astonishing nearness of heaven to earth.

Those angels are still right here—as sure as the sun.

> So we fix our eyes not on what is seen, but on what is unseen, since what is seen is temporary, but what is unseen is eternal. (2 Cor. 4:18)

PEOPLE, GET READY. JESUS IS COMING!

What If Christmas Really Started to Look a Lot Like Christmas?

LUKE 2:10–14 | But the angel said to them, "Do not be afraid. I bring you good news that will cause great joy for all the people. Today in the town of David a Savior has been born to you; he is the Messiah, the Lord. This will be a sign to you: You will find a baby wrapped in cloths and lying in a manger."

Suddenly a great company of the heavenly host appeared with the angel, praising God and saying,

"Glory to God in the highest heaven, and on earth peace to those on whom his favor rests."

Consider This

Some people hear this exalted text in the tones of Handel. I can't but help always hear it in the humble voice of Linus.

It actually takes Handel and Linus to get Christmas; angels and shepherds.

Imagine the contrast. A ragtag band of Bedouin shepherds working the night shift on the outskirts of the little town of Bethlehem and the sudden appearance of something like thousands of angelic beings surrounding them with a spectacular blinding radiance. How could it be any more contrasting?

I've always imagined all these angels hovering overhead in the sky above the shepherds. Go back and read it again. The text doesn't say they hovered overhead in the sky. It says the angels appeared to the shepherds. In every other case in Scripture, when an angel appears to someone the angel is standing before the person, not hovering above in the sky.

"So what?" you may ask. First, we need a proper picture in our minds of an angelic being. Somewhere along the way artists began depicting angels as precious little chubby babies with wings (and in the recesses my mind, I think they are holding candy canes). For starters, that's not cute. It's creepy. Come on, fat, naked babies with feathered wings hovering around in the sky? Creepy. Who thought of that?

About the closest present-day image I can conjure up that gets anywhere close to what biblical angels are like is Thor on steroids when he was already on steroids. Seriously, angelic beings are fierce, powerful, towering, terrifying creatures.

We get our first glimpse in Genesis when Adam and Eve are exiled from the garden of Eden: "After he drove the man out, he placed on the east side of the Garden of Eden cherubim and a flaming sword flashing back and forth to guard the way to the tree of life" (3:24).

And remember that time in the garden of Gethsemane when Jesus, about to be arrested, told his disciples to put away their swords, saying, "Do you think I cannot call on my Father, and he will at once put at my disposal more than twelve legions of angels?" (Matt. 26:53). (Twelve legions equals about seventy-two thousand.)

To face an angelic being would certainly mean fearing for one's life. Now, picture in your mind tens of thousands of these celestial creatures, brighter than the sun, completely surrounding these humble shepherds, not flying overhead, but standing on the ground. (Can you say, "Holy Heavenly Host, Batman!") Somewhere along the way I also got the sense these angels sounded something like the Mormon Tabernacle Choir singing. Again, the text says nothing about singing. It says they were "praising God and *saying*." Did I mention that I've always heard them singing in English to the tune of Handel's *Messiah*?

I think we have it all wrong. In all our artistic, philharmonic efforts, we have domesticated these beings down to the size of our chancels and concert halls. And I can't find anywhere in the Bible where angelic beings are actually singing. It does say in John's vision that they "cried out in a loud voice" (Rev. 7:10). When the text says they were praising God, it means they were crying out with loud voices things like:

"Amen!
Praise and glory
and wisdom and thanks and honor
and power and strength
be to our God for ever and ever.
Amen!" (Rev. 7:12)

And things like:

"'Holy, holy, holy
is the Lord God Almighty,'
who was, and is, and is to come." (Rev. 4:8)

And all of this is being shouted in an unrecorded, nonhuman language. They speak in the tongues of angels. Obviously the Holy Spirit interpreted it to Luke, but it wasn't in nice Elizabethan English. And obviously the Holy Spirit gifted one or more of those shepherds with an interpretation of the language, but these are small things for God. The big thing is the colliding realities of heaven and earth breaking in on that field outside Bethlehem, announcing the singular most astonishing thing that has ever or will ever happen in the history of history and eternity: God becoming human flesh—with us—Emmanuel.

Now what if we plugged all of this imagery of an earth-shaking encounter with tens of thousands of fierce, otherworldly angelic creatures into our minds as we sing, "It's beginning to look a lot like Christmas"?

I think you are getting my point. That fat little naked baby with wings perched on top of your Christmas tree—*not* Christmas.

What if, in our Christmas Eve services, we create a five-minute spot in the order of worship, maybe while we are holding our lit candles in the air and just before we sing "Joy to the World"? As those candles are hoisted above us, we would enter into a human reenactment of the heavenly host on that first Christmas. Everyone—men, women, and children—would be charged to shout at the top of their lungs, at levels of deafening decibels, declaring over and over and over again the following words: "Glory to God in the highest and peace on earth!"

That would actually look a lot like Christmas.

PEOPLE, GET READY. JESUS IS COMING!

Hospitality—There's Always More Room

LUKE 2:6–7 | While they were there, the time came for the baby to be born, and she gave birth to her firstborn, a son. She wrapped him in cloths and placed him in a manger, because there was no guest room available for them.

Consider This

The best things in life don't often happen at the best times and under the best conditions or circumstances.

For most of the two-thousand-year history of the church, the innkeepers of Bethlehem have taken it pretty hard. I think I have always kind of blamed them for Mary's and Joseph's plight. I mean, how could they turn God away like that? (Like they even knew.) And what were they supposed to do, throw someone out of their room in order to make room for Mary and Joseph? There was not any room.

In other words, no room means no room, unless of course, someone is willing to improvise. Creativity, after all, is the art of improvisation. When faced with a no-room situation, creative people find a way to make room. They own the situation and make a plan. It's rarely ideal, yet it works. And most of the time, in retrospect, it makes for a great story.

It wouldn't be Christmas with Jesus in a neonatal intensive care unit, now would it? It wouldn't be Christmas if some anonymous innkeeper two thousand years ago hadn't gone the extra mile and made a way when there seemed to be no way.

When you think about it, that's exactly what God is like—always making a way when there seems to be no way; making room when there is no room. It's the very point of Christmas, isn't it?

From this we can learn that true hospitality is not about who you have room for, but who you are willing to make room for. It's not who you invited that tests your hospitality, but the unexpected guest. And the truth? It's the unexpected guest who proves to be the most surprising blessing. Those are the stories that matter.

I suppose it's part of the divine irony . . . nearing the end of his short life, Jesus, the one who had nowhere to lay his head, said, "My Father's house has many rooms; if that were not so, would I have told you that I am going there to prepare a place for you?" (John 14:2).

It's a good reminder to reset our sense of hospitality. Five words to live by: there is always more room.

It brings to mind that celebrated text from Hebrews 13:2: "Do not forget to show hospitality to strangers, for by doing so some people have shown hospitality to angels without knowing it."

And some have even hosted God.

Where would we be without that innkeeper? No room in the inn? Not a problem. That's who we are. It's what we do.

PEOPLE, GET READY. JESUS IS COMING!

4 Exile

ISAIAH 5:1–8, 13–17 | I will sing for the one I love a song about his vineyard: My loved one had a vineyard on a fertile hillside. He dug it up and cleared it of stones and planted it with the choicest vines. He built a watchtower in it and cut out a winepress as well. Then he looked for a crop of good grapes, but it yielded only bad fruit.

"Now you dwellers in Jerusalem and people of Judah, judge between me and my vineyard. What more could have been done for my vineyard than I have done for it? When I looked for good grapes, why did it yield only bad? Now I will tell you what I am going to do to my vineyard: I will take away its hedge, and it will be destroyed; I will break down its wall, and it will be trampled. I will make it a wasteland, neither pruned nor cultivated, and briers and thorns will grow there. I will command the clouds not to rain on it."

The vineyard of the Lord Almighty is the nation of Israel, and the people of Judah are the vines he delighted in. And he looked for justice, but saw bloodshed; for righteousness, but heard cries of distress.

Woe to you who add house to house and join field to field till no space is left and you live alone in the land. . . .

Therefore my people will go into exile for lack of understanding; those of high rank will die of hunger and the common people will be parched with thirst. Therefore Death expands its jaws, opening wide its mouth; into it will descend their nobles and masses with all their brawlers and revelers. So people will be brought low and everyone humbled, the eyes of the arrogant humbled. But the Lord Almighty will be exalted by his justice, and the holy God will be proved holy by his righteous acts. Then sheep will graze as in their own pasture; lambs will feed among the ruins of the rich.

Consider This

JOSEPH: Mary, we've got to find a place to have this baby.

MARY: I know. And all this because of Caesar's stupid census. Why couldn't we just have this baby back home? Will it always be this way for us, Joseph?

JOSEPH: I hope not. I think our fathers and mothers who lived out their lives in Babylonian exile would think we have it pretty good compared to them.

MARY: Sure, but this return from exile hasn't been all it's cracked up to be either.

JOSEPH: I think it would do us good to remember how we got expelled from our homeland. As they say, those who can't remember their past are destined to repeat it.

MARY: Wouldn't it have been something to know Isaiah? He gave it his best, didn't he?

JOSEPH: Yep, he didn't pull any punches. He gave it to them straight.

MARY: And he even sang. That song of the vineyard was powerful. God did everything possible to help our people thrive in this land, but it's like they spit in his face. God has so much patience and mercy, but when it's over, it's over.

JOSEPH: We just keep doing the same things. God blesses us. He gives us commands to protect us. We don't listen. We don't trust. We don't obey. And God finally lets us face the consequences of our failures. The exile was like a final reset.

MARY: And still he never lets go. Adam and Eve, Abraham and Sarah, Moses and those forty years of wandering, and all those horrible kings and amazing prophets. Just like Adam and Eve were expelled from the garden, our people were expelled from the Promised Land. When trust fails, everything falls.

JOSEPH: Can you imagine what it must have been like in Babylon? They desecrated our temple and reduced it to ruins. They were horrible, especially that Nebuchadnezzar. They forced our people to sing their songs as they wept by the rivers of Babylon.

MARY: Yet we have to remember Daniel, Shadrach, Meshach, and Abednego, and their unflinching trust in God. And even in exile God kept sending prophets. He never gave up on us. Floods, fiery furnaces, lions—he stuck with us.

JOSEPH: You are right. We must keep trusting, Mary, even when it seems like all hope is lost. I keep hearing what that angel said to me over and over in my head, "You are to give him the name Jesus, because he will save his people from their sins" (Matt. 1:21).

MARY: Joe! This is a stable! What are you thinking! Am I going to have to birth this baby here?

JOSEPH: Mary, it's all we've got.

MARY: Joe! Bring that manger over here. JESUS IS COMING!

PEOPLE, GET READY. JESUS IS COMING!

Merry Christmas! The Birth Story of Eternal Life

LUKE 2:15–16 | When the angels had left them and gone into heaven, the shepherds said to one another, "Let's go to Bethlehem and see this thing that has happened, which the Lord has told us about."

So they hurried off and found Mary and Joseph, and the baby, who was lying in the manger.

Consider This

Birth stories. They are all at once ordinary and spectacular; messy and majestic.

Every single person on the face of the planet was born. Okay, I know, another obvious insight. But think about it. Every single person has in common that they came into the world through birth. Everyone has a birth story.

Unfortunately, because of sin's entry into the world through our first parents and its persistence through the line of every human lineage, down to the level of every individual person, every single person on the face of the planet will have a death story.

And in between the birth story and the death story every single person on the face of the planet has a life story. And every single one of those life stories is broken.

The big question is: Do we have an eternal life story? An eternal life story is the story of the broken being made whole; gloriously whole, and refit for unending life in the presence of God, the Creator and Father of our Lord Jesus Christ.

Christmas is the birth story of eternal life. It is the birth story of Jesus. And just like us, Jesus has a death story. However, because Jesus is the story of eternal life, his life could not be held by death. In fact, by his resurrection from the dead, his life defeated death. This is the gospel:

> For God so loved the world that he gave his one and only Son, that whoever believes in him shall not perish but have eternal life. (John 3:16)

> Yet to all who did receive him, to those who believed in his name, he gave the right to become children of God—children born not of natural descent, nor of human decision or a husband's will, but born of God. (John 1:12–13)

Jesus' eternal life story not only holds the promise of reversing our death story, it holds the unimaginable possibilities of making our life story a true story of life, life, and more life.

This is why we go to Bethlehem. This is why we go from Bethlehem to tell it on the mountain.

PEOPLE, GET READY. JESUS IS COMING!

Appendix: Exercises and Family Activities

Something most of us probably never got in church was a sense of the big story line of Scripture. We got a lot of the stories (and platitudes and proof texts), but we never got *the story*. Come to think of it, many of us memorized the names of all the books in the Old Testament in order and yet we missed the Old Testament altogether. As a result, we think of the Bible primarily as two books: the one we "get" (i.e., the New Testament) and the one we don't "get" (i.e., the Old Testament). The Bible is one book. Imagine picking up any other book and starting to read it three-fourths of the way through. Who does that? Yet this is what we mostly do with the Bible. Yes, Virginia, the Old Testament is three-fourths of the Bible.

At select points throughout the reader, we have used a dialogue approach between Mary and Joseph to remember the big story into which Advent and Christmas fit. The point here is to begin Advent with a creative rehearsal of the big story and to make some connections to the gospel story in the process. Here is how it breaks down:

Day 1: Creation—In the Beginning
Day 2: The Fall—When Trust Falls, Everything Fails

With this dialogue approach, we are trying to simultaneously give the fifty-thousand-foot view of the Old Testament while making key connections with Jesus and the New Testament. If we wanted to take it up to 100,000 feet, we could bring it down to something like a five-act play: 1. Creation 2. Israel 3. Jesus 4. Church 5. New Creation. (There it is on one hand.) Notice how Jesus is the centerpiece who holds it all together.

Advent is a reset of the story, and in order to understand this we must better grasp the story line. As we proceed we will discover that throughout history God has reset the story many times, in many places, and with many people. To speak of a reset is another way of speaking of grace. The slate is cleared and another chance is granted.

Understanding our story and where we are in the story and where the story is headed is critical to understanding ourselves and the purpose of our lives and the glorious future of forever. Kids can get this if we can get it to them. There's a lifetime to delve into the mysteries and complexities of it all. Now is the time to grasp the compelling simplicity of this, the only really true story.

For best results, rehearse the dialogue dramatically as a family. It would work well if the father and the mother played the parts of Joseph and Mary. Go for it!

Family Experiments

December 1

This is a simple one, but go into a room that can be completely dark when the lights are turned off. Instruct the participants that you (or another participant you appoint) will say the words, "And God said . . ." And, in response, another participant you appoint will say, "Let there be light!" Stand by the light switch and turn on the lights on cue. When the lights come on, the first participant will say, "And it was so." Switch roles and repeat as desired. We want our children to understand something of the nature of God's power in the ability to speak new realities into existence with words. The discussion can go in a lot of directions, from marveling at the power of God's word at creation to the angel's meeting with Mary. It can also go in the direction of the power of our words to create new realities in the world as the followers of Jesus.

December 2

Remember the trust fall exercise? Try it with your children. Have them stand on a surface higher than the floor and face forward. Next, position yourself with perhaps another person across from you, to catch them when they fall. *Make sure you can catch them!* Now, instruct them that you want them to listen carefully and obey your commands. Maybe ask them to pat their head or clap their hands or shake their right arm. After establishing the rhythm, command them to fall backward. Assure them you will catch them. All they need to do is to trust you. The point of the exercise, of course, is to make the connection between listening/hearing and obedience/trust. Before they will willingly fall backward at your command, they must trust that you will be there to catch them. Relate it back to Adam and Eve's failure to listen well to God's word to them and their failure to trust and to obey.

December 3

Over the years we have put such a snow village spin on Christmas that we think Joseph and Mary must have planned it this way. Help your children understand that this is not how they would have done it. Try and make a list of all the hard things about having a baby away from home. These days doctors forbid pregnant women from travelling any distance well before the baby is to be born. Imagine how it would have been for a very pregnant Mary to ride a donkey for eighty miles, taking about a week to get there. Help them understand that God is at work in all things and in all circumstances, the easy ones and the hard ones, to bring about good for all who love him. In particular, bring to mind people in your community or circle of influence who are suffering through a really hard time at this time of year. Think of a way you might be a blessing to them this week.

December 4

Advent can be a wonderful season to sow seeds of blessing in your local community and beyond. Sit down as a family and make a list of people who are alone or might feel isolated during the holiday season. Oftentimes, elderly people who are homebound or who live in nursing facilities experience extreme loneliness. Often families with several young children at home can experience feelings of isolation. Widows and widowers. People who have recently experienced divorce. People in the hospital. With each person on the list, think of a small way your family can reach out to bless them. It could be a visit, a note, a gift card, a much-needed favor. Use your imagination and ask the Holy Spirit to guide you. Now put these things on your calendar and go do them.

December 5

Today's entry provides a good opportunity to share the message of the gospel as a family. In the famous Christmas carol "O Little Town of Bethlehem," the last verse renders the sinner's prayer in a poignant and simple way:

> O holy Child of Bethlehem,
> Descend to us, we pray!
> Cast out our sin and enter in,
> Be born in us to-day.
> We hear the Christmas angels,
> The great glad tidings tell;
> O come to us, abide with us,
> Our Lord Emmanuel!

Take some time to share with your family that because we are sinners we need a savior—that the power of sin separates us from the presence of God but that the power of grace is greater than the power of our sin. Because of Jesus, nothing can separate us from the love of God. We must confess our sin and welcome Jesus into our lives as our Savior and Lord. Below is a way you might lead your family to pray together. Perhaps repeat the prayer line by line, inviting whoever would to repeat it after you.

Father, I confess that I am a sinner. I fall short of your glory. Even more I confess, "For God so loved the world that he gave his one and only Son, that whoever believes in him shall not perish but have eternal life" (John 3:16). I believe that you died on the cross to save me from my sin and that you rose again from the dead and are alive today. I humbly ask you to be my Savior and my Lord. I pledge my life to follow and obey you that I might become like you. Come Holy Spirit and fill me with the life of God and the love of others for the rest of my life and for all eternity. I pray in Jesus' name. Amen.

December 6

So here's the assignment: make a list of all the things you usually do to be prepared for a party. Let's say it's a party to celebrate the return of Jesus? Would you add special preparations to your list? Who would you want to invite? Make a list of everyone you want to be at the party.

Now what if I told you that the only way people can get into the party is if they know Jesus? Wouldn't that make you want to introduce as many people as possible to Jesus? What if that is the only way to invite people to the party, to introduce them to Jesus? How could you get started on that today? Who will you invite?

Here's the best way to go about it. Start making your list. Then start talking (praying) to Jesus about everybody on your list. These may be the most important preparations we can make. Hang on to that list. Don't lose it. Tuck it into your Bible.

December 7

Try this brainstorming exercise. What if Jesus gave you a million dollars and asked you to use it to bless other people? How would you use the money? Be as creative and as specific as possible. For example, don't say, "Give it to the poor." Instead, share the details of how you would do it. And remember the adage, "Give a man a fish and feed him for a day. Teach a man to fish and feed him for a lifetime."

December 8

Does your family know the Apostles' Creed? It's an ancient creed that rehearses the Christian faith. Tradition has it that each of the twelve apostles contributed a phrase to the creed. Christians have been reciting it for more than a thousand years. Try reciting it together as a family. At least once a week our family recites it together on the way to school.

I believe in God, the Father Almighty,
Maker of heaven and earth;
And in Jesus Christ his only Son, our Lord;
who was conceived by the Holy Spirit,

born of the Virgin Mary,
suffered under Pontius Pilate,
was crucified, dead, and buried;
the third day he rose from the dead;
he ascended into heaven,
and sitteth at the right hand of God the Father Almighty;
from thence he shall come to judge the quick and the dead.

I believe in the Holy Spirit,
the holy catholic church,
the communion of saints,
the forgiveness of sins,
the resurrection of the body,
and the life everlasting. Amen.

December 9

The world is filled with injustice. Martin Luther King Jr. once famously said, "Injustice anywhere is a threat to justice everywhere." As a family, try to list ways you see injustice seeming to prevail in the world today. Make a list of them and agree together to present this list to God at least one day a week for the next year. Remember, we are like the powerless widow, but God is nothing like the unjust judge. Let's never give up. And let's be open to how God might guide us to respond to these unjust situations on our list.

December 10

We did a trust fall a couple of days ago. That's what I would call the breakthrough of trust. That's what it's like to put your trust in Jesus, to come to grips with the fact that only he can save us from falling. It's the kind of trust it took to walk out into the middle of the parted waters of the Red Sea, knowing they could crash in on you at any time but trusting that God would deliver them through it.

Today we are going to try a trust walk. Trust calls for a big leap of faith at the beginning, yet it requires a long process of following Jesus after that. We learn to walk by a trusting faith and not by mere eyesight.

Get a blindfold and put it on a child. Now turn the child around a few times to disorient their sense of direction. Try the first half of the walk with the child behind you, holding your belt or shoulder as you lead them through obstacles and around corners and such. In the second half of the walk, you will walk beside them, giving them detailed and clear instructions on how to move forward without being able to see. This works best outdoors where you have to walk through tight spaces and under low-hanging limbs and across rough patches of ground and around trees. It can also work inside. Get a bunch of plastic cups and/or balls of different sizes and scatter them across an open room with a chair here and there. The adult talks the blindfolded child from the starting line through the obstacles without touching any and on to the designated finish line. After doing this, switch up the roles and have the adult wear the blindfold.

This exercise makes tangible the need to listen carefully and to demonstrate complete trust by following directions all while having no ability to find one's way alone. This is what God taught Israel in the desert years. This is how Jesus guides our steps through the Holy Spirit throughout our lives. Keep remembering the big story!

December 11

As we have discussed these past several days, Advent is as much about the second coming of Jesus as it is about his first coming at Christmas. Go outside as a family and gaze upon the clouds. Try to imagine and envision Jesus appearing on a cloud and coming toward the earth. What would that be like? If you would like to take it a step further today, take the whole family to a cemetery. Gather together out in the middle of the place and read today's text, 1 Thessalonians 4:16–18, aloud. Talk about what that will be like.

December 12

Take a few minutes as a family to talk about repentance. The word literally means to turn around, making a 180-degree turn and walking in the opposite direction. Ask your children to walk in a straight line toward one end of the room, instructing them to turn and walk in the opposite direction when they hear you say the word, "Repent." Talk about what this means when it comes to our thoughts, actions, and behavior.

December 13

Today presents us with a verse crying out to be rememberized: "But seek first his kingdom and his righteousness, and
all these things will be given to you as well" (Matt. 6:33).
Try writing it in a prominent place in your home, perhaps
a chalkboard. (For more on the meaning of "rememberize,"
see page 38.)

December 14

Today is a good day for an antiphonal refrain. Practice the
one from today's text: ask one member of the family to say,
"The Lord lifts up," and everyone else says, "those who bow
down." Give every member of the family permission to start
the litany anytime and in any place. The only rule is that
when one person says it everyone else has to repeat the rest
of it. For good measure, during your family devotion time
today invite everyone to bow down—to get down on their
knees—and pray together. Finish the prayer time by saying
the Lord's Prayer together.

Here are a few more Advent antiphonal refrains for good
measure:

Luke 1:46–47
Leader: My soul magnifies the Lord
Family: And my spirit rejoices in God my Savior.

Psalm 127:1
Leader: Unless the Lord builds the house
Family: Those who build it labor in vain.

Isaiah 40:8
Leader: The grass withers and the flowers fall
Family: But the word of our God endures forever.

December 15

Families get hundreds of opportunities every single day to put the interests of others ahead of their own. On one occasion, Jesus taught that whoever wanted to be the greatest must become the servant and that the last would actually be the first. Most often, the name of the game is to see who can be first. Seeking the kingdom of God means just the opposite. Begin a contest in your family to see who can be last the most. Who can "out-last" the others? Figure out a way to celebrate and reward efforts at "out-lasting" one another. You will be surprised at how this changes things.

December 16

"I once was lost but now I'm found, was blind but now I see." "Amazing Grace," the famous hymn, tells us the basic story of the power of the gospel of Jesus Christ. The gospel doesn't just save us, it changes us. That's what today's Scripture text is all about. The point of the gospel is not getting our souls into heaven (though that is a good thing). The bigger point is getting heaven into our souls. Take a few minutes to fill in these blanks, "I once was _____ but now I am _____," and share the story with your family. Invite others to share as they are willing. Invite everyone to fill in the blanks as they want it to be in the future too. This will give you all good leads on how to pray for and encourage one another.

December 17

Tomorrow we will deal with the consequences of the failure of Israel's kings: exile. I want you to ponder all these connections. I want you to marvel at the way this story holds together with such intricacy. You've probably already made the connection between that donkey carrying Mary carrying Jesus and the donkey who will later carry Jesus into the city of Jerusalem—David's throne. No wonder we call him the King of kings. God is resetting the story line not by throwing out the past but by reincorporating it, bringing it all to fulfillment in Jesus. He does the same with our lives. He resets the story line of our lives not by throwing out our past but by redeeming it, bringing it all to fulfillment in Jesus. Amazing grace.

These connections are probably difficult for children to make. What's most important is your making them—for yourself. This is the stuff of God. This is the heart of worship. Treasure these things and ponder them in your heart.

December 18

One way of fixing our eyes on Jesus is to talk about him together. As a way of doing just that, today let's play the, "My favorite thing about Jesus is . . ." game. It can be a favorite quality or character trait or story he told or thing he said or, or, or . . . you get the point. Appoint someone to be the recorder. Even better, crank up the voice recorder on your smart phone and capture it like that. It just might become a family treasure.

December 19

Who knew Advent would be so much about repentance? And all this time we thought it was about *pa rum pum pum pum!* Down through the centuries Advent has always been a season to contemplate a closer walk with Jesus and this always means repentance. It is so critical for us to grasp that repentance is about loving other people. Love is the armor of light. Too often we think of repentance only in the terms of what we are turning away from. It is equally if not more important to give attention to what or who we are turning to. Talk about this as a family today. How can turning away from sin be translated practically into turning toward love? Lead the way in the sharing. Your vulnerability will give others courage.

December 20

Today brings us to another text worthy of rememberizing. "Trust in the Lord with all your heart and lean not on your own understanding; in all your ways submit to him, and he will make your paths straight" (Prov. 3:5–6).

December 21

Get ready for a mind-blowing conversation with the family today. Discuss the difference between invisible and un-seeable. Ask someone from the family to hide behind the couch or to stand on the other side of a door or a wall where they cannot be seen by everyone in the room. Now ask the question, "Is (name) invisible?" The answer is no. They have just become un-seeable. When we say something or someone is invisible we are saying something about that person. When we say they are un-seeable we are saying something about us. It is impossible to see that which is invisible. We need only eyes to see or a different vantage point to see that which is un-seeable. See the difference? Here's the kicker. So what if Jesus and heaven and the angels are not invisible? What if they are just un-seeable? Most often these days it's children who report seeing angels. Given all this, what would it mean for us to be on the lookout in a whole new way? What if all that we presently perceive as un-seeable is not somewhere up there but right here in our midst? I warned you.

December 22

Okay, it's time to get our imagination on. It's time for the Radiant Angelic Being Drawing Contest. Pass out paper, pencils, and so forth and go for it. What do you think one of those angels looked like? Roasted chestnut to the winner! Or a candy cane—winner's choice!

December 23

Okay family, it's time to sing. Let each member of the family choose their favorite Christmas carol and then sing at least the first verse of each song together as a family. P.S. "Grandma Got Run over by a Reindeer" doesn't count!

December 24
Be sure and go to church today or tonight. Even if you don't regularly go to church, go to church. Even if you never go to church, go to church. Christmas Eve is for church, and yes, Santa Claus, but more so, it's for church. And if you can't go to church, do church at home. Sometimes those can be the sweetest celebrations of all.

December 25
Merry Christmas!!!

Advent Ideas from the Field
At Seedbed we love to learn how people are sowing the grace of God out in the fields of their everyday lives. We put out an open invitation (which remains open) for others to share their ways and means of doing Advent as a family. Several of them are included below. Please send us yours at farmteam@seedbed.com.

> Dear Seedbed,
>
> One thing that we do during the Advent season is put our Christmas cards in a box on our kitchen table. Each night after supper we pick a card and pray for the family. Our four boys sometimes fight over which family to pick. We talk about the family and we each

spend time praying for them. We send that family a postcard saying that the Jones family prayed for them this week. We've been doing this for six years and we love it. We usually go well into the year praying for families.

The Jones Family
Hattiesburg, Mississippi

Dear Seedbed,

As a single person, I know I don't necessarily qualify as a family with an Advent tradition. However, I do have a few traditions I share with families:

1) I always purchase my niece, nephew, two godchildren, and the pastor's son the chocolate calendar from Divine Chocolates. It's always got the nativity in the artwork along with some way of describing the process of chocolate from cacao bean to delicious heart. Also, when each box is opened, the flap tells another simple aspect of the nativity story. The kids are now middle school ages with one freshman in high school—they do expect this from their auntie, but they also report (and I see the evidence)—that they do limit themselves to one candy a day and they take turns reading the flaps aloud.

2) Also, I purchase a few extra calendars that I use when I teach at a Christian college—I am able to share about fair trade and a little about Advent traditions. Since most of the students are from Pentecostal

and other non-denominational backgrounds, it is interesting to discuss with them the meaning of the liturgical year.

3) I make it a habit to shop for Advent at Christmas—pick up books, devotionals, coloring pages, crafts, and candles when they go on discount. I will share with particular families I know the next year. Several years ago, a friend/colleague overseas took in Christian refugees who were missing their Christian community in Syria and I had a nice package to send to a family I didn't know that particular year.

4) Listen to Advent music, specifically to about December 15. I have a few CDs but also have an Advent station on Pandora.

5) Make a new Advent wreath with fresh greenery, pinecones, and other natural pieces, as well as purple and pink ribbons each year. I also have a little brass angel calendar I bought with my Nana for $0.15 (yes, that is supposed to be 15 cents!) when I was a very little girl at a church bazaar. When I light each candle on each wreath each Sunday, I play meditative music from George Winston's album *Winter*.

6) Try out different daily devotionals. I try to keep up with the lectionary reading each day. After all, I haven't ever bought myself the chocolate calendar, so I don't have flaps to open and read, but I find the daily lectionary reading to help tell the story and bring me to a place in which I do become expectant for Jesus'

coming—remembering it in Nazareth but also awaiting its fulfillment for our world. This future orientation of Advent helps set the tone for me that there is an expectant time in awaiting.

Grace and peace,
The Grimm Family
Chesterfield, United Kingdom

Dear Seedbed,

So here's our Advent tradition: we stuffed a strand of colored LED Christmas lights into an old mason jar (leave the lid off). When the girls go to bed each night, instead of our usual story time we turn off all the lights and gather around the jar and read from the Jesus Storybook Bible. If you start with creation on the first day of Advent, you get to Jesus' birth by Christmas. It's kinda cool because it tells the whole story. We call it . . . wait for it . . . the Advent Jar.

The Al-Rikabi Family
Heath, Texas

Dear Seedbed,

My parents started this tradition with my siblings and me. We'd light the Advent wreath together and read the brief liturgy. After we remembered what God was doing in sending Jesus, we shifted to family celebration. Mom would pull out some of the Christmas cookies she'd already baked, we'd have snacks, and pick a Christmas movie to watch together. The Sunday nights of Advent became sacred family time in a very busy season. The shining Advent wreath burned while we dimmed the lights and had this sweet family time. When I got married my parents gave me a special Advent wreath for my family. We're carrying on the tradition while the other members of our family celebrate across the miles. I love knowing we're all connected as we celebrate Advent apart each Sunday night.

The Wanck Family
Washington, Illinois

Dear Seedbed,

We have a large green poster board tree cutout, and we have twenty-five red circle ornaments with different names of Jesus on them. We put one ornament on each day at dinner and try to talk about what each name signifies and why Jesus would be called that name (Wonderful Counsellor, Lamb of God, etc.). We also have an Advent playlist that we keep on in the background during the entire season.

The Donald Family
Foley, Alabama

Dear Seedbed

We sing Advent hymns at bedtime and other times. (No Christmas hymns till Christmas!!)

We wear purple. :)

We had a Christmas Cookie Exchange party, but instead of taking cookies home, we delivered them to refugee families who recently settled in Lexington.

We have collected hats and scarves for refugees.

When our kids were younger, we read through the Jesus Storybook Bible during Advent.

We celebrate Christmas for twelve days—this makes waiting for it better!

The Merricks Family
Wilmore, Kentucky

Dear Seedbed,

Acts of service for others, volunteering (Salvation Army bell, food drive, etc.).

Putting together nativity set.

Scripture box of Advent verses to pull from and read at meals.

Empty manger under the tree.

Reading Advent or Christmas books at night.

Practicing hospitality and involving kids in preparation and hosting, sharing.

The Nader Family
Arlington, Texas

Dear Seedbed,

We keep it pretty simple. We built a basic framework for families to do together each evening during this time.

Light a candle.

Read a text.

Sing a song (or listen to a song).

Pray.

(Then blow the candle out.)

Here's a link to how we led people to do this last Advent. We also give each family a candle in our worship gathering the Sunday before Advent.

It has been amazing to see how this simple thing has become huge for so many families. We've heard stories from many families who had never read the Bible together—fathers who had never prayed in front of their kids, kids offering profound and prophetic things, and just a lot of fun.

For our own family, it's become a great season. Our kids love it—even as they get older. Some nights Leslie and I are tired and just want to get the kids to bed but they say, "Are we going to do Advent tonight?" We make small things a big deal. They take turns lighting the candle, take turns reading each night, picking out their favorite song (we usually just create a playlist of good songs), then take turns blowing out the candle. We dim the lights when we do this, talk softer, lean in toward each other—all usually fresh from showers and baths and in pajamas. It's a holy moment. Building wonder in them. But it's also light, fun and not too serious.

Aside from this we also do an Advent calendar. It's a calendar for December, but we turn it into an Advent one. Each day the star moves closer to the 25th. But each night we put three Hershey kisses in the pouch for the next morning—along with a note of something special. The next morning the kids get up, head to the calendar to get a Hershey kiss, and read something like,

"Tonight, hot coco during our Advent time" or "Sonic run after school today" or "Candle light dinner tonight." We just take simple things that are not hard and build them into big deals for the kids during Advent. This just builds anticipation and wonder of the season.

The Agerton Family
Auburn, Alabama

Dear Seedbed,

Our family tried the Lego calendar one year and got the complete opposite of Advent from our kids. It was an epic fail. Last year was the best family integration we've had so far. With a seven-, five-, and two-year-old this year, we'll see how it goes.

Our rhythms:

—We read one chapter of the Jesus Story Book Bible each night (roughly twenty-five to Jesus' birth).

—We bless our neighbors by baking goods for them and/or spending time with them as we are able, making room for them as guests and friends.

—Our Advent prayers close with "Maranatha," and we talk about what it means for heaven to come to earth.

—We look for ways to bless and sacrifice for others in tangible ways. Usually for our kids that means giving up favorite toys or sharing favorite things with others.

The Causey Family
Lawrenceberg, Kentucky